We Learn All About
Transportation

A Complete Resource
for Preschool, Kindergarten,
and First Grade Teachers

by Sharon MacDonald

Fearon Teacher Aids
Simon & Schuster Supplementary Education Group

Editor: Marilyn Trow
Copyeditor: Kristin Eclov
Illustration: Pauline Phung
Design: Diann Abbott

ISBN 0-8224-4592-1

Printed in the United States of America
1.9 8 7 6 5 4

Contents

To the Teacher

Dear Teacher:

In this book you will find everything you need to introduce transportation into your classroom. It is a complete unit packed full of background information and learning activities that will help you teach children about transportation.

The materials are presented in four sections—About Transportation, Land Transportation, Water Transportation, and Air Transportation. You can pick and choose which topics you want to use. Each section contains an *introduction* and *activities*. The introductions give the basics of the topics, so there is little need for you to gather additional information on transportation. The activities suggest projects for art time, snack time, play time, and learning time that correspond to and reinforce the topics. Since there are a number of activities listed for each topic, you can choose the ones that are appropriate for your class's skill level.

The *suggested reading* at the end of the teacher's guide lists reading and picture books that will enhance the children's enjoyment of transportation. I suggest that when you introduce a topic, you also read one or two of the books to the children. You could also leave out picture books for the children to look at on their own.

The eleven reproducible *worksheets* incorporate thinking and concept skills such as visual-discrimination skills and the fine-motor skills of drawing, cutting, and pasting. Suggestions for using the worksheets and the eight reproducible *pattern pages* are included with the activities.

Have fun bringing transportation to your classroom!

Sincerely,

Sharon MacDonald

TEACHER'S GUIDE

About Transportation

INTRODUCTION

Transportation is an important part of our lives. Transportation means moving people or goods from place to place. From the past to the present, different types of transportation have been used to help make people's lives better.

Land transportation has changed from goods being carried by people to goods and people being transported by cars, buses, trucks, and trains. Dugout canoes and rafts made from logs are two of the earliest ways of moving people and goods across water. Today ships, submarines, and boats provide a much faster and safer way of transporting people and goods across waterways. Air transportation has seen dramatic changes over the years—from hot-air balloons to airplanes and jets. Recent developments in space travel promise to open up even faster and more exciting transportation opportunities.

Transportation is used for both work and play. The type of transportation used by people depends upon where they live. In the United States, many families use cars, trucks, and vans. Animals, ships, planes, and trains are also popular forms of transportation. Children rely upon wagons, bicycles, scooters, and skateboards for transportation and fun.

Each type of transportation depends on energy. People and animals need food for energy. Cars, trucks, planes, trains, and ships use gasoline, diesel, and nuclear energy. Scientists are experimenting with other forms of energy for use in transportation as well, such as the sun, wind, and water. New forms of moving people and goods continue to be perfected to meet people's ever-changing and growing needs.

ACTIVITIES

 Place several large building blocks on the classroom floor. Help the children brainstorm different ways to move the blocks. Invite the children to try some of the methods they suggest. Then ask children how they think food and clothing get to grocery and department stores. Explain that when goods and people are moved from place to place, this is called *transportation*. Duplicate and hand out Worksheet 1 (page 23). Discuss each picture on the handout. Then have the children match each picture with the appropriate form of transportation. Suggest that interested children draw pictures illustrating other uses of transportation vehicles as well.

About Transportation

ACTIVITIES

 Point out that transportation can be used for work and play. Help the children brainstorm a list of different types of transportation—bicycles, cars, trucks, trains, ships, scooters, roller skates, and so on. Write each transportation word on a strip of tagboard. Title a bulletin board "We use transportation for. . . ." Divide the bulletin board into two sections. Title one section "Work" and the other section "Play." Help the children pin each word strip on the appropriate side of the bulletin board as you read aloud each word. Encourage the children to find pictures in magazines or draw pictures to pin next to each strip. Invite children to add pictures of other types of transportation to the bulletin-board display.

 Make a transportation activity bulletin board. Design a background scene that includes roads, rivers, and sky. Use construction paper and the pattern pages provided on pages 37-44 to create a variety of vehicles that move on land, water, and through the air. Trace the vehicles onto the construction paper and cut each vehicle out. Punch a hole near the top of each vehicle. Place the vehicles in an envelope. Staple the envelope to the bulletin board. Encourage children to arrange the vehicles on the board.

 Invite the children to share stories about family vacations or other places they have visited. Ask the children how they traveled to each place—by car, train, airplane, bus, and so on. If you have children in your classroom from other countries, encourage these children to share information about ways people and goods are transported in their homelands.

About Transportation

ACTIVITIES

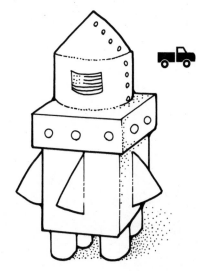

 Help the children brainstorm some fun vehicles. Provide a variety of large rectangular and square boxes, cardboard tubes, and other containers. Invite the children to use the boxes to design their own vehicles. Suggest that children use tempera paint, construction paper, and other attachable accessories to make their vehicles attractive. When the children finish, give each child (or group of children) a copy of Worksheet 2 (page 24). Have the children draw pictures of their vehicles and then decide whether the vehicles will be used on land, water, or in the air. Invite each child (or group of children) to show his or her vehicle to the rest of the class and explain its use.

 Make a display showing several different types of transportation. Use both pictures and models. Encourage children to design vehicles from play dough. You may use the recipe for play dough provided here. Use masking tape to map off "roads" on the play dough table. Then invite the children to enjoy dramatic play with each completed play dough vehicle.

Play Dough Recipe

1 cup flour	$^1/2$ cup salt
1 tbsp. oil	1 cup water
2 tsp. cream of tartar	food coloring (optional)

Mix together all the ingredients in a bowl. Pour the mixture into an electric skillet and cook at 350° until the mixture is a solid lump. The mixture will pull away from the sides of the skillet into a firm ball. Knead the dough until it cools and then store in a covered plastic container.

If possible, bring several miniature toy cars to school. Pour tempera paint into small, flat paint trays. Use several different colors. Set two cars in each tray. Invite the children to roll the wheels of the cars through the tempera paint and then across large sheets of manila paper. Encourage the children to make tracks using a variety of colors. Display the completed car track designs in the classroom.

About Transportation

ACTIVITIES

 Cut out magazine pictures of vehicles powered by air, gasoline or diesel engines, and people. Glue the pictures to tagboard and then cut out each picture. If possible, laminate each picture for durability. Tape the pictures to wooden blocks for children to use in the block area.

Encourage the children to discuss the following questions. Write their responses on chart paper. Then have children draw pictures to illustrate their favorite responses.

What might happen if an airplane flew on the highway?
What might happen if a ship tried to fly?
What would probably happen if a bus tried to drive across a lake?

Show the children various pictures of land, water, and air transportation vehicles. Help the children categorize each picture. Duplicate and hand out copies of Worksheet 3 (page 25). Have the children cut out the vehicle pictures and glue them to the appropriate sections on their worksheets.

Land Transportation

INTRODUCTION

There are many different types of land transportation. The most common land vehicles are cars, buses, trucks, and trains. Cars are used to move small groups of people long or short distances. People rely on cars for work and play.

Buses can carry more people than cars. School buses take children to and from school. Special motor coach buses take people to other cities and parts of the country.

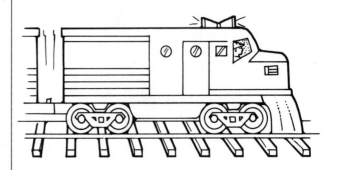

Land Transportation

Trucks have many uses. Special refrigerated trucks carry food to grocery stores. Dump trucks are used to haul dirt, sand, and rock. Garbage trucks help keep cities clean. Moving vans help people move their furniture and other belongings to new homes.

Trains are another type of land transportation used to move people and goods from place to place. Trains have many different sections, called cars. Train cars are pulled along a track by a large engine. Tons of coal are moved in cars called hoppers. Box cars transport animals and farm products. Trains can even carry automobiles.

ACTIVITIES

Encourage the children to observe a well-traveled street from a school window. Or take the children on a class walk to a very busy street. Point out the variety of vehicles seen on the streets and sidewalks. When you return to the classroom, have available various sizes of rectangles, squares, circles, and triangles cut from construction paper. Invite the children to design land vehicles using the different shapes. Have the children assemble and then glue the parts on background sheets of construction paper. Suggest that children use markers to add roads, buildings, and other details.

Read *The Little Engine That Could* by Watty Piper (Buccaneer Books, 1981). Invite the children to dramatize the story using the train patterns provided on pages 37-38 and building blocks. Duplicate the patterns and color them. Glue the patterns to tagboard and then cut out each train car. Tape each railroad car to a block. Arrange colored tape on the floor in the block area to represent railroad tracks. Then invite the children to slide the play railroad car blocks along the tape tracks.

Invite a semi-truck driver to come visit the classroom and share information about his or her job with the children. Ask the driver to show the semi-truck and trailer to the children. If possible, arrange for the children to experience sitting in the driver's seat and standing inside the large trailer. Help the children write a thank-you letter to the driver a few days after the school visit. Duplicate and hand out Worksheet 4 (page 26). Have the children connect the dots and color the picture. Include the children's drawings with the thank-you letter.

Land Transportation

ACTIVITIES

Take the children outside to observe a garbage truck picking up the garbage in the school dumpster. Encourage the children to discuss where garbage trucks take the garbage every day.

 If possible, arrange for the children to take a short ride in a school bus. Discuss bus safety. Point out the special safety features on the bus. After the ride, show the children how to draw a bus using only rectangles, squares, and circles (see below). Encourage the children to experiment with other ways of drawing a bus using a variety of shapes.

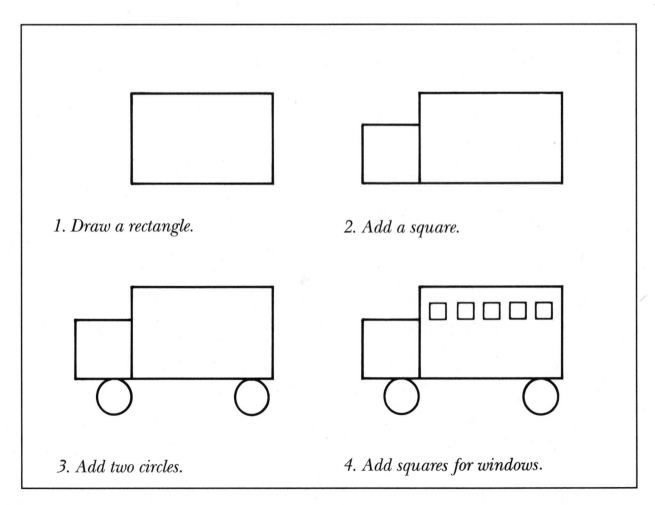

1. Draw a rectangle.

2. Add a square.

3. Add two circles.

4. Add squares for windows.

Land Transportation

 Invite the children to role-play car safety. Suggest that children pretend they are going to the store. Help the children talk through the situation as they role-play ("First, we pull the handle and open the door. . ."). Duplicate and hand out Worksheet 5 (page 27). Encourage the children to cut out the pictures and sequence them first, before gluing them to the numbered squares.

Collect several small toy cars, trucks, and buses for use in the sandbox. Help the children arrange the vehicles by categories. Then duplicate and hand out Worksheet 6 (page 28).

Display several old license plates in the classroom. Point out that each car, truck, and bus must have a current license plate before it may be driven on the streets and highways. Help the children make license plate rubbings. Show the children how to place lightweight paper over the plates and then rub a crayon gently over the paper. Discuss the differences between the various plates.

Bring a tricycle or other wheeled vehicle to school. You might invite the children to bring tricycles from home as well. Set up an obstacle course on the playground or in a large area of the classroom. Encourage safe "driving."

Use the patterns provided on pages 39-40 to make tagboard stencils of land vehicles. Have the children trace the different land vehicles on sheets of construction paper. Use the vehicles to make a large wall collage.

Collect a variety of old car keys. Trace the keys on sheets of tagboard. Place the keys in a container. Then invite the children to select a key and match the key to its tagboard silhouette.

Land Transportation

ACTIVITIES

 Cut vehicle shapes from easel paper. Invite children to paint the shapes at the painting easel.

 Duplicate and hand out Worksheet 7 (page 29). Have the children complete the shape pattern in each row.

Water Transportation

INTRODUCTION

Water transportation is another important way to move people and goods from place to place. Ships are some of the oldest kinds of water transportation. Huge tankers haul oil and other fuels. Cargo ships carry everything from cars to children's toys. Passenger ships called ocean liners carry people. Battleships are used by the armed forces to carry soldiers and supplies across the ocean. Carrier ships actually have runways on which airplanes may land and take off.

Submarines are built to move both on and under water. A submarine has a periscope for observing things above water while the submarine is actually below water. Submarines are powered by special engines that allow them to move fast underwater, just as other types of ships move quickly along the surface of the water.

Tugboats have the important job of pulling big ships and tankers to dock. Ferries take people and cars across narrow spans of water. Coast guard rescue boats help people in boats when they are in trouble.

Boats are generally used on rivers, lakes, and ponds. Some boats are powered by motors and others are powered by the wind blowing on sails.

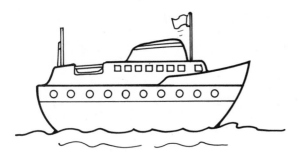

Water Transportation

 Set up a water play area outside or in the classroom. Fill a large plastic tub with water. Provide a variety of plastic boats for children to sail in the water. Invite the children to share boats from home for use in the water center as well. Encourage children to experiment using wind, water currents, or their hands as the power source to move the boats.

 Set up a "Sink or Float" science activity center. Place a small tub of water on a table. Put a variety of objects that will sink and a variety of objects that will float in a container by the tub. Place two trays on the table. Glue a picture of an item that will sink on one tray and a picture of an object that will float on the other tray. Cover the pictures with contact paper or laminate them for durability. Write the words "Sink" or "Float" on each tray as well. Encourage the children to work independently or in small cooperative learning groups to test the objects to see if they sink or float. After each object is tested, have the children place the object on the appropriate tray.

 Invite the children to design boats using pieces of styrofoam, twigs, craft sticks, and triangular-shaped pieces of plastic. When the boats are completed, have the children test them at the water table or sink.

Invite the children to draw underwater pictures. Spread a thin coat of blue fingerpaint on a large tray and invite the children to make designs in the paint with their fingers. When a child finishes fingerpainting, carefully press a sheet of paper over the design. The picture will transfer onto the paper. You may need to add more paint to the tray before the next child takes his or her turn. Display the designs in the classroom. Show the children pictures of oceans, rivers, and lakes. Help the children compare their designs with actual underwater pictures.

Water Transportation

ACTIVITIES

 Make a boat from a large refrigerator box. Use stiff cardboard pieces for paddles. Provide real life jackets. Discuss the need for boat safety. Ask the children to share experiences they may have had with boating. Then invite small groups of children to take imaginary boat rides. Remind them to role-play the boat safety rules discussed in class. Then duplicate and hand out Worksheet 8 (page 30).

 Set up a "Let's Go Fishing" center in the classroom. Make magnetic fishing poles from old broom handles or dowel sticks. Tie a long piece of string to one end of each stick and attach a heavy magnet to the other end of the string. Cut out fish shapes from different colored poster board. Glue a large paper clip to each fish. Letters or numerals may be printed on the fish to encourage visual discrimination. Invite the children to use the magnetic poles to "catch" particular fish. If the refrigerator boat in the previous activity is made, you might spread the fish on the floor surrounding the boat and invite the children to "fish" from the boat.

Place five different size plastic boats on a tray. Help the children arrange the boats in order according to size. Encourage the children to group the boats in other ways as well—by color, shape, use, and so on. Duplicate and hand out Worksheet 9 (page 31).

If possible, display a model of a submarine (or show the children a picture of a submarine). Point out the various parts of the submarine and explain their uses. Duplicate and hand out Worksheet 10 (page 32). Have the children color the numbered spaces to reveal a yellow submarine.

Water Transportation

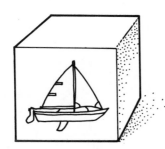

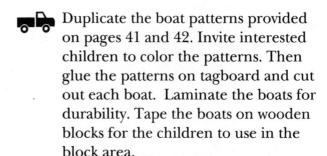

Duplicate the boat patterns provided on pages 41 and 42. Invite interested children to color the patterns. Then glue the patterns on tagboard and cut out each boat. Laminate the boats for durability. Tape the boats on wooden blocks for the children to use in the block area.

Air Transportation

INTRODUCTION

Air transportation is the fastest way to move people and goods from place to place. Air transportation is sometimes the only way to get to places when there are no roads, rails, or water that would allow travel by other means.

Airplanes can be small with one engine. These planes can carry only a few passengers. Jetliners are large airplanes that carry hundreds of passengers and tons of luggage. These airliners can fly four hundred fifty to six hundred miles per hour because they have powerful jet engines to move them forward and large wings to give them lift.

A remarkable invention of modern times is the helicopter, sometimes called a whirlybird. Helicopters can fly straight up and down, backwards and forwards, and sideways. Some carry only one person, while others can easily carry thirty people. Special helicopters can lift very heavy

objects weighing up to six tons. Helicopters are used for air-sea rescues. Large companies often use helicopters to move products to remote places that have no roads or runways. Hospitals use helicopters to transport injured and sick people to other medical centers. The helicopters actually land on the roofs of the hospitals.

Air Transportation

ACTIVITIES

 Ask the children if they have ever flown on an airplane. Encourage the children who have flown to share their experiences with the rest of the class. Invite the children to dramatize boarding an airplane. Arrange the chairs in rows with a central aisle. Make tickets printed with seat numbers. Tape corresponding seat numbers to the chairs. Have the children get their tickets and then find their seats by matching their ticket numbers with the seat numbers. If this activity is done during snack time, you might assign one or two children to role-play a flight attendant to serve snacks on trays (styrofoam meat trays work nicely).

 If possible, arrange to take the children on a field trip to a nearby airport. Special tours are available at most airports through the public relations office. When the children return to the classroom, encourage them to discuss what they saw and learned. Have the children draw pictures of their favorite parts of the trip. Invite each child to dictate a sentence or two about his or her picture as you write what is said on the picture. Then include these drawings with a thank-you letter to the tour guide.

 Encourage children to bring to school toy airplanes, helicopters, or other aircraft to share with the class. You may also make a set of aircraft toys. Duplicate the patterns provided on pages 43-44. Make multiple copies of each type of air transportation. Color the patterns and then glue them to tagboard. Laminate the patterns for durability. Cut out each vehicle and tape to wooden blocks. Help the children sort the aircraft according to types. Count the number of items in each set. Encourage the children to classify the vehicles using other criteria as well.

Obtain a cardboard box large enough to hold a child (a washing machine or dishwasher box). Use the box to make a helicopter. Cut cardboard pieces for the propeller blades. Attach the blades to an old broom stick (the propeller shaft). Cut a hole in the top of the box. Insert the shaft. Then invite the children to take turns "flying" the helicopter by sitting inside the box, grasping the end of the propeller shaft and rotating it to simulate flying.

Air Transportation

ACTIVITIES

 Make peanut butter play dough. A recipe is provided here. Invite the children to make their own individual batches. Be sure to have the children wash their hands first. Then encourage the children to use the dough to form various aircraft shapes. When they are finished, invite the children to eat their creations!

Peanut Butter Play Dough

1 cup peanut butter
1 cup powdered milk
$^{1}/_{2}$ cup honey

Mix together all ingredients. Makes one batch.

 Sponsor a "Rocket Launch." Thread a plastic drinking straw on a long string. Tie each end of the string to opposite walls in the classroom. Slide the straw to one end. Inflate a balloon. Hold it shut tightly with one hand and tape it beneath the straw with the other hand (the top of the balloon pointing in the direction the rocket will be traveling). Have the children count backwards from the number ten. As the children say "zero," release the balloon by letting go with your hands. The balloon rocket will "fly" across the room along the string.

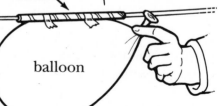

straw

balloon

ACTIVITIES

Make sky pictures. Mix liquid starch and glitter in a jar. Invite the children to use the mixture to paint on large black sheets of paper at the easel. When the mixture dries, the starch will disappear leaving the glitter to represent the stars and planets in the evening sky. Encourage children to color and cut out pictures of airplanes to glue on the sky pictures as well.

Duplicate and hand out Worksheet 11 (page 33). Have the children match the numeral to the number of aircraft on each line.

Suggested Reading

Barton, Byron. *Airplanes*. New York: Crowell, 1986. Other books in this series: *Boats, Trains,* and *Trucks*. (PS-K).

Billout, Buy. *By Camel or by Car: A Look at Transportation*. New York: Treehouse, 1983. (1-3).

Burningham, John. *Mr. Grumpy's Motor Car*. New York: Penguin Press, 1983. (1-3).

Crews, Donald. *Freight Train*. New York: Greenwillow Books, 1984. (K-3).

Crews, Donald. *School Bus*. New York: Greenwillow Books, 1984. (K-3).

Gibbons, Gail. *Boat Book*. New York: Holiday House, 1983. (PS-3). Other books in this series: *Fill It Up* (K-4), *New Road!* (K-4), and *Trains* (PS-3).

Graham, Margaret. *Benji's Boat Trip*. New York: Harper & Row, 1977. (PS-3).

Gramatky, Hardie. *Little Toot*. New York: Putnam Publishing Group, 1978. (K-2).

Ingoglia, Gina. *The Big Book of Real Airplanes*. New York: Putnam Publishing Group, 1987. (1-4).

Lenski, Lois. *The Little Airplane*. New York: MacKay, 1980. Other books in this series: *The Little Auto, The Little Train,* and *The Little Sailboat*. (K-3).

Piper, Watty. *The Little Engine That Could*. New York: Buccaneer Books, 1981. (PS-1).

Rockwell, Anne. *Things That Go*. New York: E. P. Dutton, 1986. (PS-1).

Rockwell, Anne. *Trucks*. New York: E. P. Dutton, 1984. (PS-1).

Scarry, Richard. *Richard Scarry's Cars and Trucks and Things That Go*. New York: Golden Books, 1974. (PS-2).

STUDENT WORKSHEETS

Name _____

Which vehicle would you use? Trace each
dotted line without lifting your pencil.

To go to a friend's house?

To cross a lake?

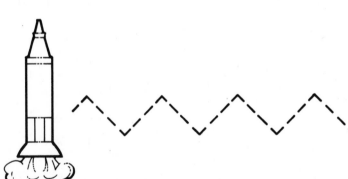 

To go to the moon?

To get the fruit to market?

Skills: fine motor (drawing)   23

_____'s Vehicle

name

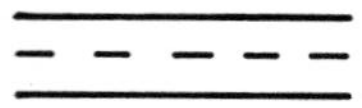

My vehicle will go

on land   on water   in the air

Skills: fine motor (drawing)

We Learn All About Transportation © 1991 Fearon Teacher Aids

Name

Cut and then paste each picture in the correct box.

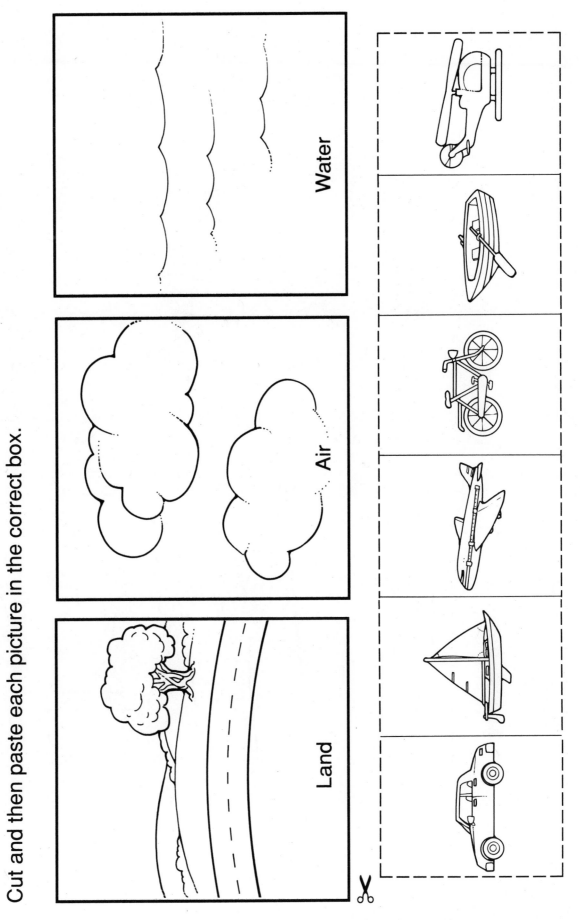

Water

Air

Land

Skills: fine motor (cutting and pasting), classifying

25

Name _____

Connect the dots in order from A to Z.

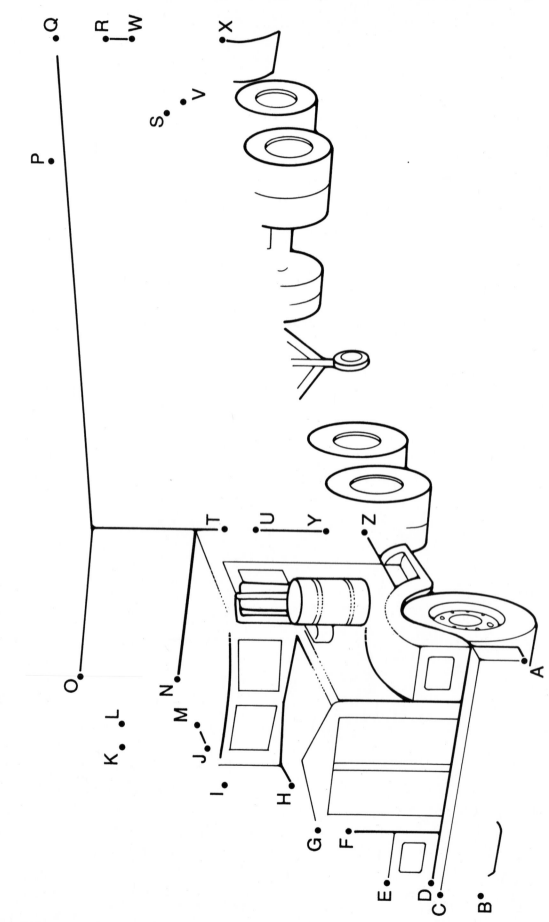

Skills: alphabetizing letters, fine motor (drawing)

Name _____

Cut and then paste the cards in the correct order to tell a story.

1	2
3	**4**

✂ -

Pull the handle.

Buckle up and close the door.

Open the door.

Take a ride.

Skills: sequencing, fine motor (cutting and pasting)

Name _____

In each row, find the ones that match. Color them
the same.

Skills: understanding the concept of same, visual discrimination

Name _____

Look at each row. Find the pattern. Cut and then paste the picture that completes each pattern.

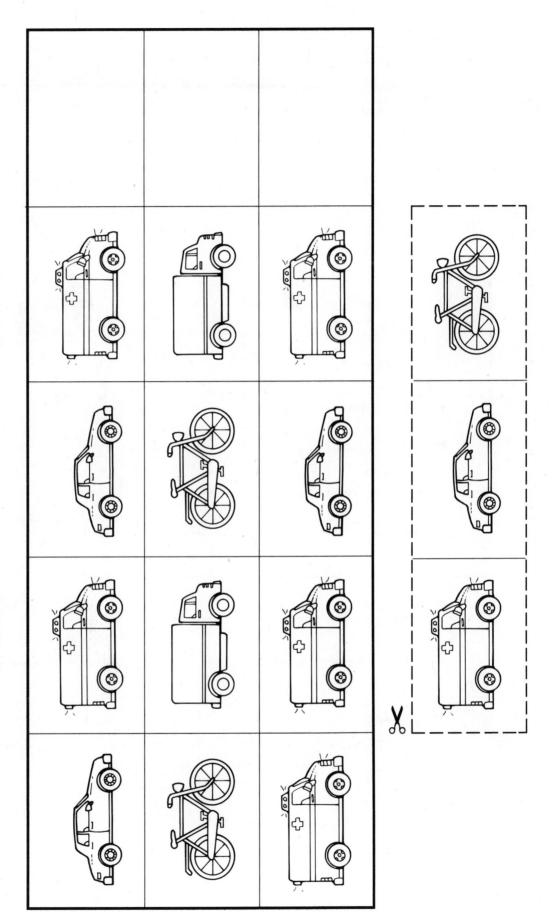

Skills: sequencing, visual discrimination, fine motor (cutting and pasting)

Name _____

Help the fisherman reach a good fishing spot. Do
not cross any lines.

Skills: fine motor (drawing)

We Learn All About Transportation © 1991 Fearon Teacher Aids

Name _____

Connect the dots in order from 1 to 25.

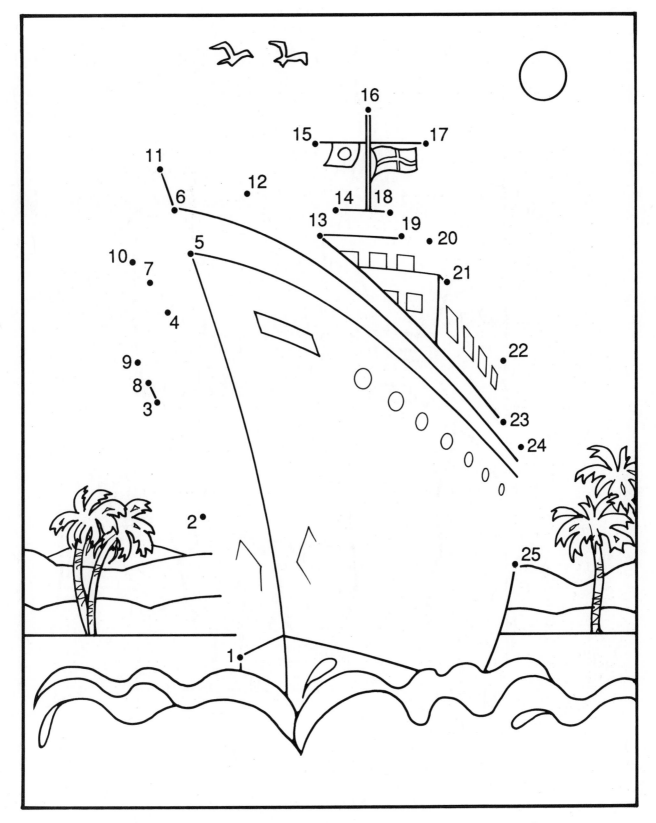

Name

Color the spaces these colors.
1 = yellow
2 = blue

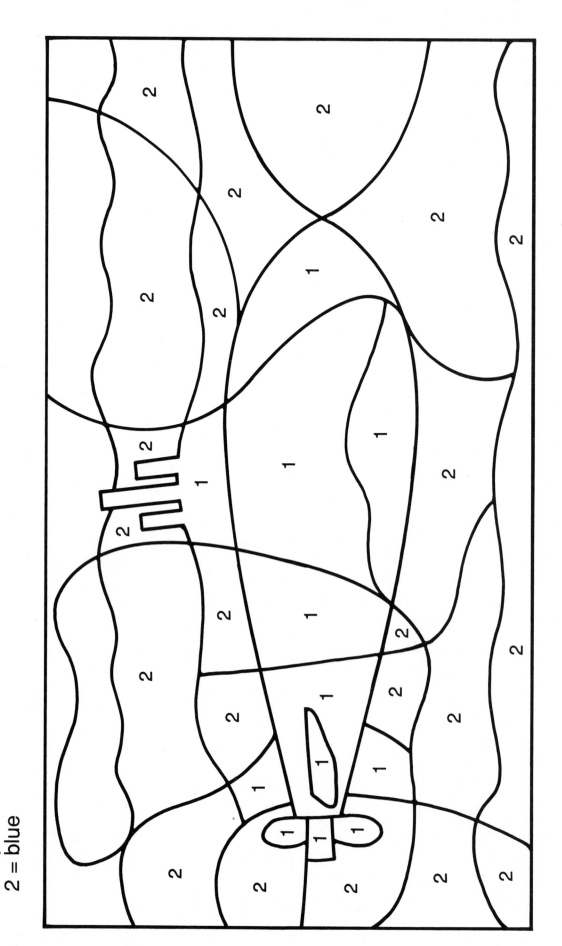

Skills: number and color recognition

We Learn All About Transportation © 1991 Fearon Teacher Aids

Name _____

Count the vehicles in each row. Paste the correct number in each box.

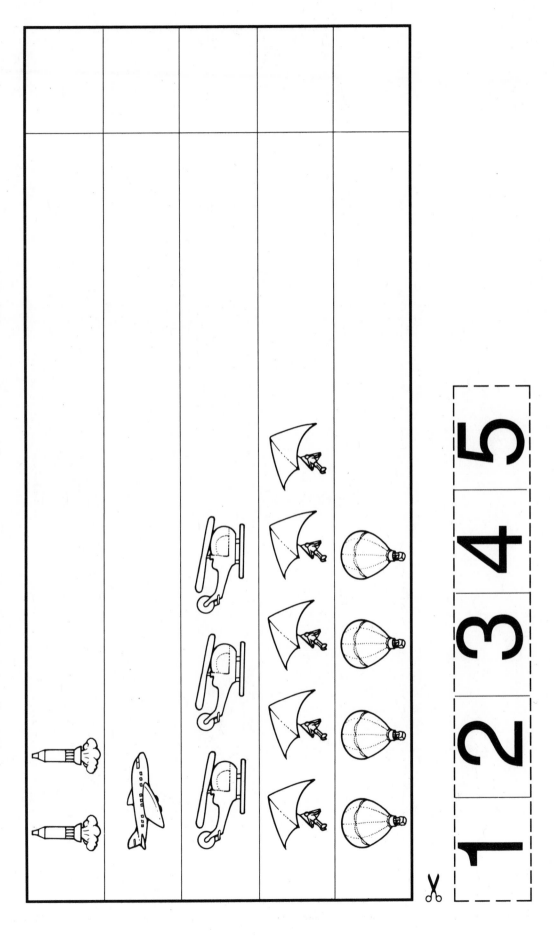

Skills: counting to 5, understanding numeral values, fine motor (cutting and pasting)   33

PATTERN PAGES

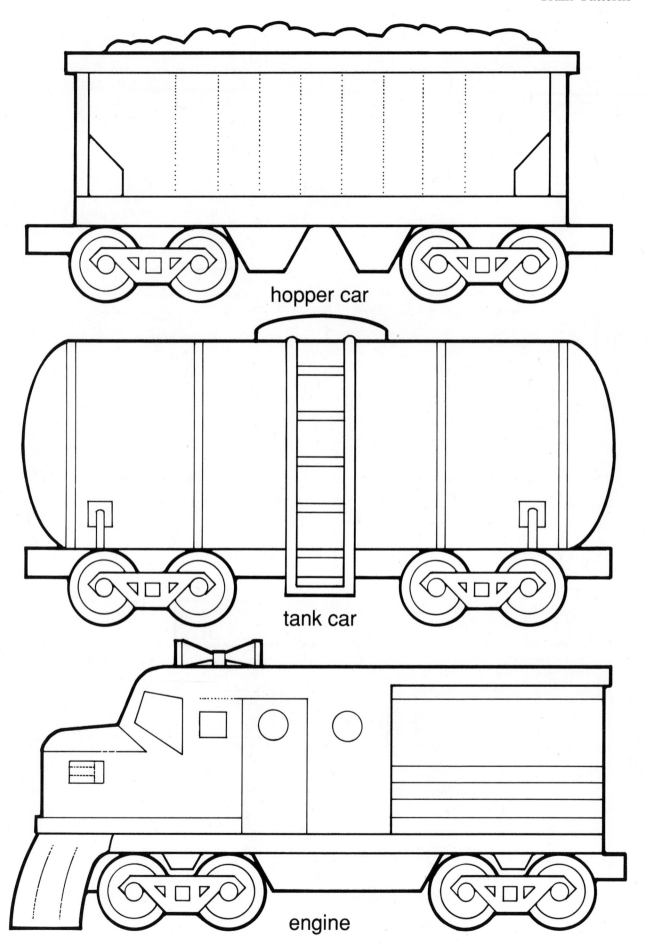

hopper car

tank car

engine

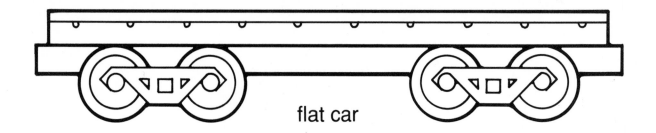

flat car

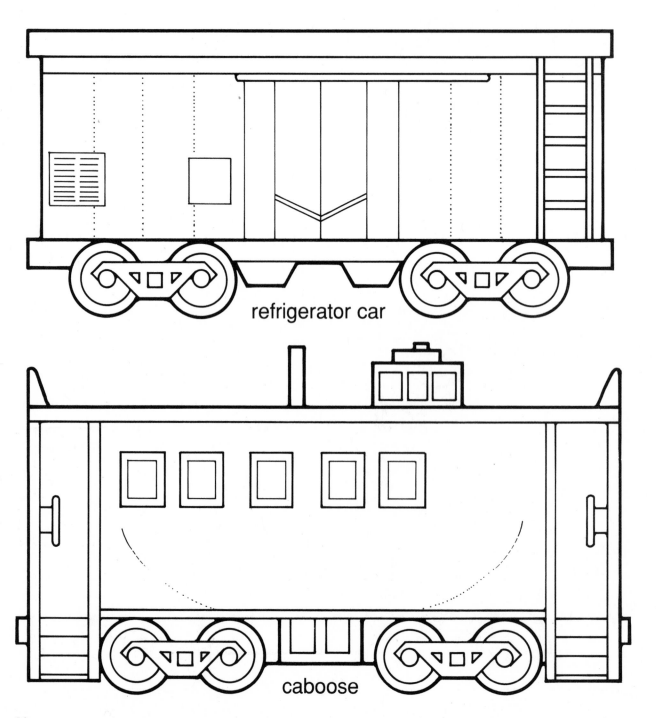

refrigerator car

caboose

We Learn All About Transportation © 1991 Fearon Teacher Aids

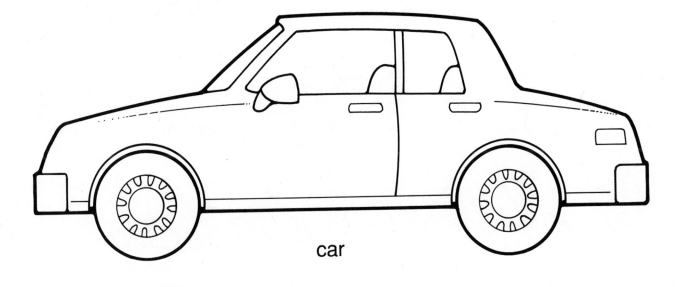

car

AMBULANCE

police or emergency van

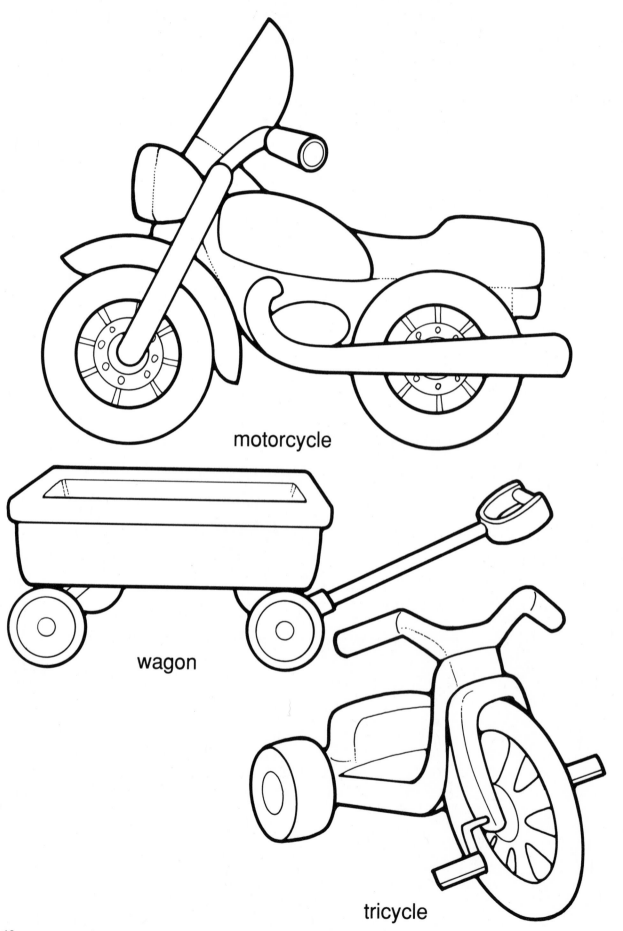

motorcycle

wagon

tricycle

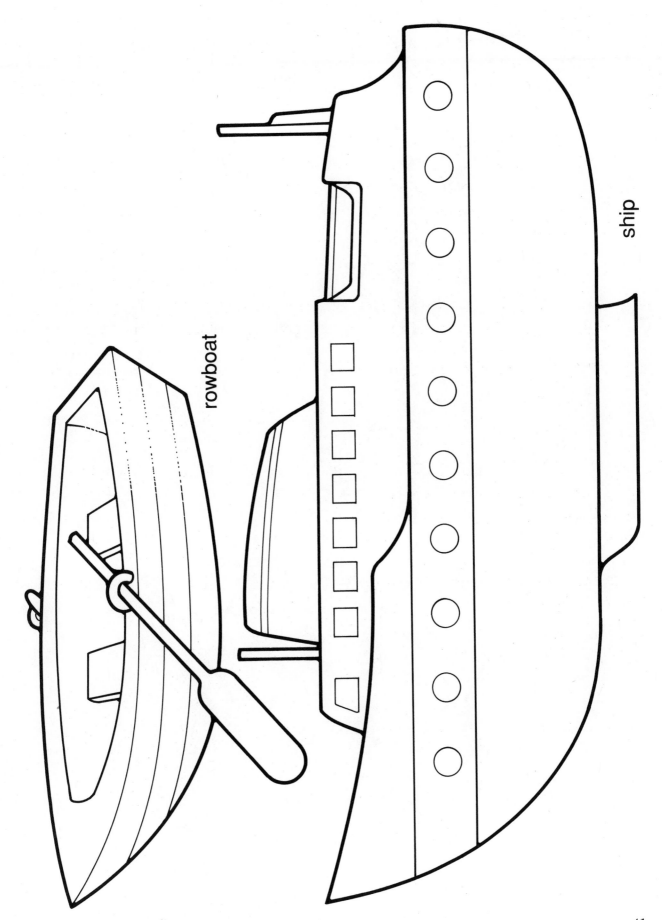

ship

rowboat

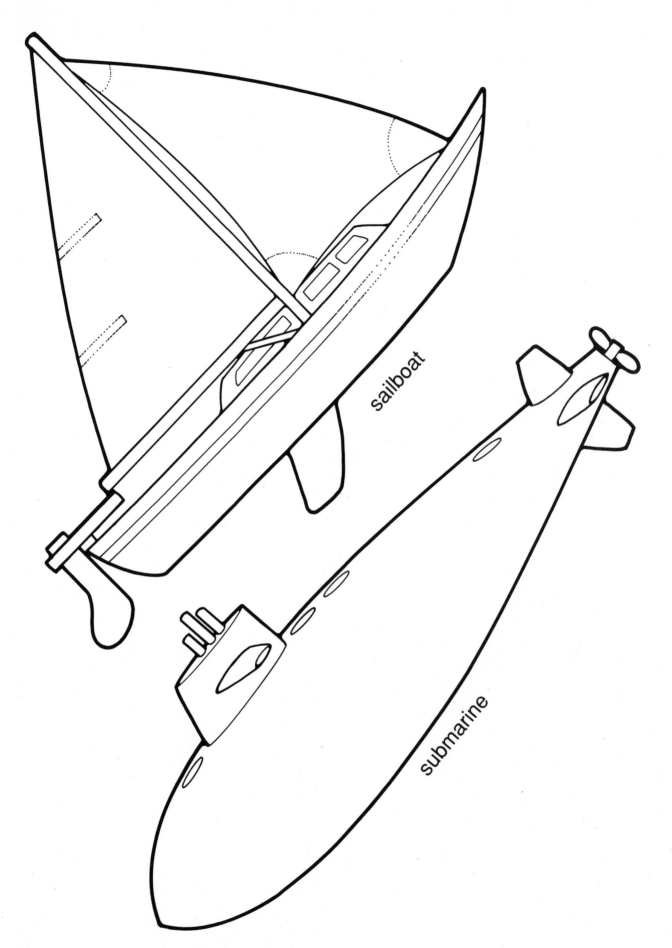

sailboat

submarine

hot-air balloon

airplane

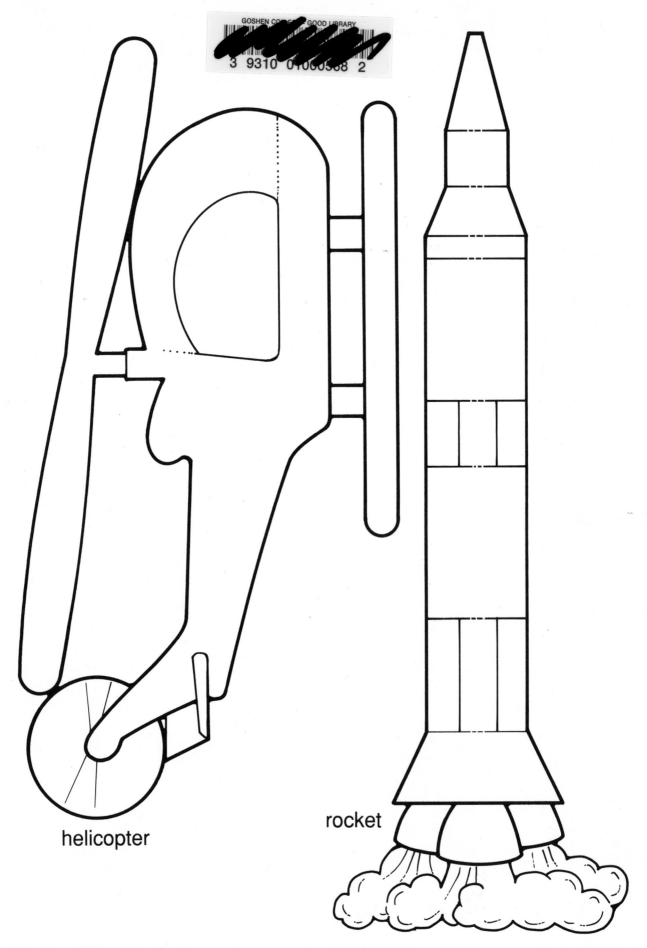

helicopter

rocket

We Learn All About Transportation © 1991 Fearon Teacher Aids